Siberian Huskies

by Grace Hansen

Abdo Kids Jumbo is an Imprint of Abdo Kids
abdobooks.com

abdobooks.com

Published by Abdo Kids, a division of ABDO, P.O. Box 398166, Minneapolis, Minnesota 55439.
Copyright © 2022 by Abdo Consulting Group, Inc. International copyrights reserved in all countries.
No part of this book may be reproduced in any form without written permission from the publisher.
Abdo Kids Jumbo™ is a trademark and logo of Abdo Kids.

Printed in the United States of America, North Mankato, Minnesota.

052021

092021

Photo Credits: iStock, Shutterstock, Thinkstock, ©Andrea Reis Photography p.5

Production Contributors: Teddy Borth, Jennie Forsberg, Grace Hansen
Design Contributors: Dorothy Toth, Pakou Moua

Library of Congress Control Number: 2020947525
Publisher's Cataloging-in-Publication Data

Names: Hansen, Grace, author.

Title: Siberian huskies / by Grace Hansen

Description: Minneapolis, Minnesota : Abdo Kids, 2022 | Series: Dogs | Includes online resources and
    index.

Identifiers: ISBN 9781098206048 (lib. bdg.) | ISBN 9781098206604 (ebook) | ISBN 9781098206888
    (Read-to-Me ebook)

Subjects: LCSH: Siberian husky--Juvenile literature. | Working dogs--Juvenile literature. | Dogs--Juvenile
    literature. | Animal behavior--Juvenile literature.

Classification: DDC 599.772--dc23

Table of Contents

Siberian Huskies

Siberian huskies are as outgoing as they are loyal.

The Siberian husky's **ancestors** were **bred** in Asia by the **Chukchi** people. The Chukchi people kept these dogs as family members and tough sled dogs.

The **Chukchi** people were semi **nomadic**. They moved from place to place, especially to hunt. They needed a dog that could haul heavy loads in very cold temperatures.

From these dogs came the Siberian huskies we know and love today. In the early 1900s, husky teams won many dog sled races. They caught the attention of people everywhere.

Siberian huskies are medium-sized working dogs. They are known for their beautiful fur coats and bright eyes.

Their ears stand up straight.

Their eyes can be brown or blue.

They can sometimes have one

eye of each color!

Grooming

Huskies are naturally clean. They only need to be bathed every 3 months or so. They should be brushed regularly to keep their coats healthy.

Exercise

Siberian huskies are energetic and athletic. It is important that they get lots of exercise. Born to run, they are happiest doing that with their owners.

Personality

Pack dogs by nature, Siberian huskies love their families and other pets. They are a great addition to any team!

More Facts

- A husky's almond-shaped eyes allow the dog to squint to keep the snow out while running. Its thick, double coat keeps the dog nice and warm.

- Huskies are heroes of history. In 1925, children living in Nome, Alaska, became very sick. They needed medicine that was hundreds of miles away. It was decided that multiple dogsled teams would get the medicine to Nome.

- Two famous Siberian huskies on that life-saving run were Balto and Togo. Balto is more well-known. He ran the last 55 miles (89 km) to Nome. But Togo and his team ran the most dangerous leg of the journey. Togo's musher said, "I never had a better dog than Togo."

Glossary

ancestor – an early type of animal from which others have evolved.

bred – developed over time for a certain purpose.

Chukchi – indigenous people inhabiting the northeastern most part of Siberia in Russia.

loyal – showing devotion and faithfulness to someone.

musher – one who travels with a dog team.

nomadic – living in a group or tribe that moves from place to place.

Index

Abdo Kids
ONLINE
FREE! ONLINE MULTIMEDIA RESOURCES

Visit **abdokids.com** to access crafts, games, videos, and more!

Use Abdo Kids code **DSK6048** or scan this QR code!